THE TATRA
NATIONAL PARK

Wiesław Siarzewski

THE TATRA NATIONAL PARK

The Tatra National Park
Zakopane 2006

Text and editing
Wiesław Siarzewski

Photography
Jan Chmiel (57); lookGaleria/Delpho (61); lookGaleria/F. Hecker (62); lookGaleria/M. Hoefer (62);
lookGaleria/C. Huetter (74); Piotr Krzywda (8); lookGaleria/D. Kurz (48); Edward Lichota (okładka);
Zbigniew Ładygin (33, 44, 45, 52, 53, 65, 66, 72, 74, 78); lookGaleria/Mertsch (48);
lookGaleria/Sailer-Schnizler (48); Wiesław Siarzewski (9, 10, 11, 12–13, 16,
23, 24, 26–27, 28, 29, 31, 32, 34, 38, 40, 41, 42, 44, 45, 46, 50, 52, 53, 54, 55, 56, 58, 59,
60, 63, 64, 65, 66, 67, 68–69, 70, 72, 76, 77, 80); lookGaleria/H. Schmidbauer (48, 74);
Tomasz Skrzydłowski (42); Zdeno Vlach (14); Edward Walusiak (45); Ewa Zarębska (44);
Filip Zięba (37, 39, 47, 48, 62, 73); Feliks Zwierzchowski (6); Tomasz Zwijacz Kozica (49, 74)

Translation by
Sigillum Sp. z o.o.

DTP
lookStudio
ul. Walerego Sławka 3A, 30-633 Kraków, Poland
tel./fax (+48 12) 655 53 74
e-mail: biuro@lookgaleria.pl, www.lookstudio.pl

© Copyright Wydawnictwa Tatrzańskiego Parku Narodowego
ul. T. Chałubińskiego 42a, 34-500 Zakopane, Poland
tel. (+48 18) 20 23 200; e-mail: sekretariat@tpn.pl, www.tpn.pl

ISBN 83-85832-80-7

List of contents

Dear Tourist　　　　　　　　　　　　　　　　　　　　　　　7

Background　　　　　　　　　　　　　　　　　　　　　　9

  I. History of the exploration of, threats to and the protection of the Tatras　　19

II. Inanimate nature　　　　　　　　　　　　　　　　25
  Geological structure　　　　　　　　　　　　　　25
  Land relief　　　　　　　　　　　　　　　　　29
  Caves　　　　　　　　　　　　　　　　　　31
  Climate　　　　　　　　　　　　　　　　　36
  Waters　　　　　　　　　　　　　　　　　40

III. Flora and fauna　　　　　　　　　　　　　　43
  The sub-alpine forest belt　　　　　　　　　　51
  The dwarf mountain pine belt　　　　　　　　64
  The mountain pasture and fell belt　　　　　　67

IV. The historic and present threats　　　　　　　75

Bibliography　　　　　　　　　　　　　　　　79

Dear Tourist,

Welcome to the Tatra National Park, one of the most beautiful mountain regions of Poland. Please bear in mind that you are just one among the millions who visit our Park every year. Remember about your safety in the mountains and protect their unique nature. When entering the Tatra National Park, please observe its rules and in particular remember that:

– you must stay on marked roads and tourist trails in the Tatra National Park;

– organised groups may visit the Tatras only with licensed Tatra guides;

– skiing is allowed only on alpine skiing slopes, marked ski-routes and designated skiing areas;

– the whole natural environment is protected within the Tatra National Park;

– you must not damage or remove rocks, minerals and other natural specimens from the Park;

– all plant and animal species found in the Park are protected, not only those subject to species protection in the whole territory of Poland;

– do not pick flowers, berries or mushrooms;

– do not disturb wild animals;

– do not create noise;

– do not leave litter – take your trash with you;

– do not camp or light bonfires;

– park your car in a guarded car park;

– dogs are not permitted.

Should you find yourself in trouble in the mountains, ask other tourists, park employees or the mountain rescue service for help. We hope you will find much pleasure in mountain hiking, viewing the Tatra landscape, the unique vegetation and animals and will return many times to the Tatras in the future. You are invited to our Education Centre and the Tourist Information Office of the Park at the Kuźnickie Roundabout in Zakopane.

Background

The Tatra region is the highest mountain massif of the Carpathians. It constitutes a small part of a huge Central European mountain chain which stretches over a distance of more than 1,300 km and occupies an area of some 209,000 km^2. The Tatras form a part of the Inner Western Carpathians. Their area amounts to approximately 785 km^2, of which only 175 km^2 lies on Polish territory. The Tatra massif is clearly defined in it surroundings, but is only 57 km long and slightly over 18 km wide. The length of the main Tatra range from the Huciańska Pass in the west to the Zdziarska Pass in the east is approximately 80 km. In this relatively small distance, the elevation above sea level changes from some 900 m at base level to 2655 m at Gerlach – the highest Tatra peak – and 2499 m at Rysy, the highest peak of the Polish Tatras.

The tallest peaks in the Polish part of the Eastern Tatras: Niżnie Rysy and Rysy

Western Tatra landscape: Czerwone Wierchy

The Tatras cover only 0.56% of the area of Poland and are the only Polish fragment of alpine high mountain landscape, with a varied geological structure and land relief as well as a great diversity of other natural features.

The Polish Tatras can be divided into two structurally distinct parts: the southern part made of crystalline rocks – granitoids in the east and of metamorphic rocks in the west – and the northern part, made up of sedimentary rocks of the *wierchy* (summit) and then the *regiel* (nappe) units. This rock layout leads to a belt arrangement of all the environmental elements. The crystalline part has the highest relative and absolute heights. It is character-ised by postglacial erosion relief, with numerous tarns as the greatest landscape attraction of the eastern part of the Tatras: the largest being Morskie Oko covering almost 35 ha, and the deepest Wielki Staw in the Pięciu Stawów Polskich Valley with a depth of over 79 m. The *wierchy* part of the Tatras is lower and features a high-mountain karst relief and underground water courses. Its great natural attraction consists in the numerous caves, over 700 of which have so far been explored in the Polish Tatras. The nappe part has the character of a highland and is cut in the eastern and western part by transit river valleys which connect the higher parts of Tatras with their hinterlands. In those valleys, postglacial moraines are found. The remaining, middle part of the nappe belt bears no traces of glaciation and has a relief typical of areas shaped mainly by river water (fluvial relief).

The geological structure and land relief contribute to the differentiation of the remain-ing natural environmental features. They have had a significant impact on the surface and underground water flows in the Tatra massif and have created specific habitats for plants and animals. All the abiotic elements of the natural environment, which are arranged in belts, and the climate, which is vertically differentiated, i.e. changes at different elevations above sea level, have had a decisive impact on the spatial and altitude ranges of the biotic environmental elements – the plant cover and animals.

Landscape of the nappe part of the Tatras: the Bystra Valley

The belt layout of the vegetation, different ways in which plants and animals have adjusted to alpine life as well as the occurrence of rare, endemic and relic species found nowhere else make the Tatras very attractive for naturalists and tourists. This attraction is further strengthened by the fact that compared to other alpine-type mountains, the Tatra area is very small, and is therefore easily accessible.

Because of the natural differentiation, three meso-regions are distinguished in the Polish part of the Tatras: the Nappe Tatras, the Western Tatras and the Eastern Tatras, widely referred to as the High Tatras.

The Tatra National Park (Polish abbreviation: TPN), established under a Regulation of the Council of Ministers dated 30 October 1954, started its activities on 1 January 1955. Since May 2003, a new Regulation of the Council of Ministers on the Tatras has been in force. The main purpose of the Park is to study and protect the natural resources of the Polish Tatras. The Park also fulfils a number of social functions (including scientific research, tourism, sports, recreation and cultural heritage protection) as well as unquantifiable functions (e.g. creative inspiration, natural education and spiritual uplifting of society) which are subordinate to the purpose for which it has been established and are therefore subject to various limitations imposed by the current legal regulations.

The area of the Tatra National Park amounts to 21,164 ha, making it one of the largest national parks in Poland. The entire Polish part of the Tatras and almost 3,700 ha of forests directly to the north of these mountains lie within the perimeter of the Park. The Park is located in the Małopolska Province, in the Zakopane, Kościelisko, Poronin and Bukowina Tatrzańska communes. In 2003, a buffer zone of over 180 ha was established in the Zakopane commune on land adjoining the Park. Across the state border to the south, east and west, the Park neighbours on the Slovak Tatras National Park (TANAP). Over 87% of the Park area (18,479 ha) belongs to the State Treasury, the rest is owned by forest partner-

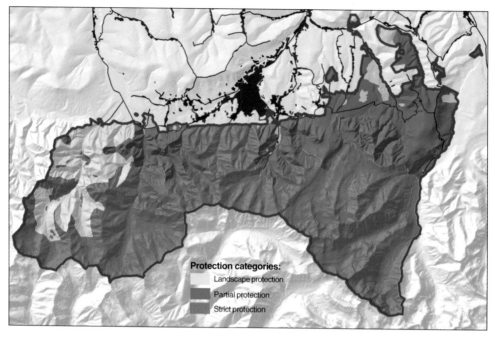

Map 1. Protective zoning of the Tatra National Park

Inside tower mountain forest zone

ships, private individuals and other owners. Some 70% of the park area is covered with forests and dwarf mountain pine brushwoods, while mountain pastures, rock and water occupy the remaining 30%. Almost 12,000 ha of the Park represents areas under passive (strict) protection, which include the entire belt of mountain pastures and fells, the dwarf-pine belt and parts of the upper and lower sub-alpine forests. In these areas, all processes taking place in the environment are protected, which in practice should ensure zero human interference in the condition of the ecosystems and natural elements. Areas under the active (partial) protection account for over 6,100 ha in the Park. They include mainly lower sub-alpine forests which have been strongly transformed by human use in the past. In these forests, the ecosystems and elements of the environment are actively protected to restore them to their natural condition or maintain them in a condition similar to natural. Over 2,700 ha of the Park area is subject to landscape protection. This area includes land owned by the Forest Commonwealth of 8 Empowered Villages with its offices in Witów, owned by the State Treasury and managed by the Park, managed by other entities, and land transferred for perpetual usufruct, where various traditional forms of management are applied.

The Tatra National Park is available for tourism, climbing, cave exploration and skiing. It has a well developed, permanently marked network of tourist trails totalling some 250 km. These trails are of different difficulty levels, ranging from walking paths to routes for experienced mountain walkers. Six caves are open to tourists and are accessible via marked trails. Biking is also permitted on four specially marked roads and trails between 1 May and 30 November. A fee is charged for entering the Park. Well developed tourist facilities are available in the immediate vicinity of the Park, in Zakopane and the surrounding villages. In the Tatras themselves, there are 8 mountain lodges open year-round, and at the perimeter of the Park there are 4 car parks and 2 other parking facilities. Tourists visiting the Park may travel by horse-drawn carriages/sleds along four marked routes.

A cable railway to the peak of Kasprowy Wierch, chairlifts and other ski lifts provide facilities for downhill skiing. Skiing is allowed on some 160 km of ski routes and trails as well as on meadows next to several mountain lodges. The periphery of the Park contains a well developed infrastructure for competition skiing: ski jumps, a slalom course and cross-country skiing tracks.

Climbing and cave exploration are also permitted in the Tatra National Park. Climbing routes have been designated for climbers affiliated to the Polish Mountaineering and Climbing Federation (PZA) and several dozen caves have been designated for sports and training activities by cave explorers. Climbing and mountaineering courses are organised in the Tatras at the training centre on Hala Gąsienicowa.

Scientific research is also permitted in the Tatra National Park. However, to conduct research activities, scientists need the permission of the Park Director, which may be granted if all the conditions imposed by the current regulations are fulfilled. Scientists and students may use the specialist library of the Park and the documentation of research previously conducted here. The employees of the Scientific and Education Department can assist them in developing professional relations with other specialists conducting research in the Tatras.

The Tatra National Park runs an education centre specialising in educational activities for teenagers. It organises classes for primary and secondary school students, trips for groups of specialists, as well as regular competitions in the knowledge of the Tatras and their region. This centre co-operates with other institutions from the Podhale region which provide similar educational services, including schools and culture centres. The centre also

The offices of the management and the education centre of the TPN in Zakopane

offers a permanent museum exhibition allowing the visitor to learn about the nature of the Tatras, the history of its protection and current developments in the Park.

In addition, the centre holds temporary exhibitions on subjects related to the Tatras, nature protection and the culture of the Podhale region. Its auditorium is used to screen nature films about the Tatras, as well as organise slide shows, lectures and training activities from time to time. The education activities of the Park are not limited to the centre only. Within the Park, there are two education nature trails (to Morskie Oko and around the Białego Valley), and classes are also organised in the Tatra botanical garden surrounding the Park management building. Finally, the centre organises meetings with Park employees for primary and secondary school students.

The Tatra National Park Tourist Information Office at the Kuźnickie Roundabout sells various publications about the park. One can also obtain information about the current conditions for touring the Tatras there.

The management offices of the Tatra National Park are located at the following address: Zakopane, ul. Chałubińskiego 42a, tel. (+48 18) 20 23 200; tel./fax (+48 18) 20 23 299, e-mail: sekretariat@tpn.pl. The same building houses the education centre and the Park museum.

Information about the Tatra National Park and current details about access to it are available on the Park website – http://www.tpn.pl

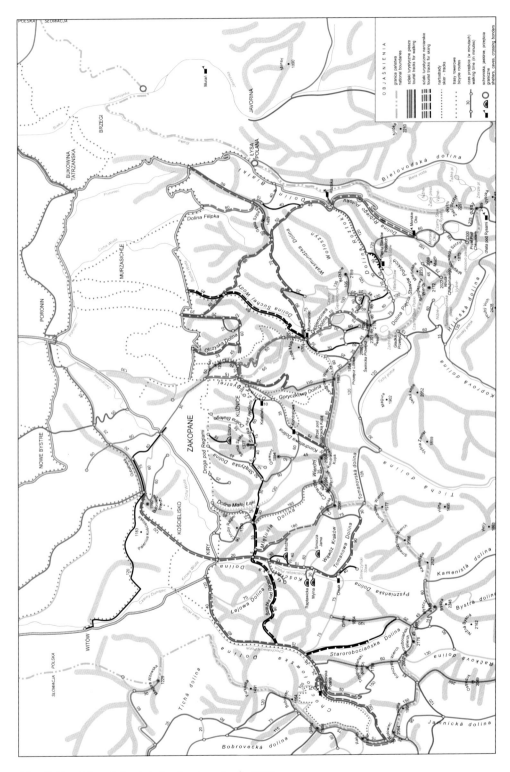

Map 2. Tourist and sports infrastructure in the TPN

Shepherding in the Tatras in the late 19th century, a drawing by W. Eljasz

The Kuźnice Zakopiańskie iron works around 1860 based on a photograph by W. Rzewuski

I. History of the exploration of, threats to and the protection of the Tatras

The oldest surviving documents show that exploration of the Tatras began in the Middle Ages. Probably as early as the turn of the 13th and 14th centuries, semi-nomadic herdsmen from nearby settlements led their herds of goats, sheep and cattle to some clearnings and mountain pastures on the southern Tatra slopes. At the same time, the more accessible valleys were explored by gold and precious stone prospectors. At the foot of the Krywań Mountain, in the vicinity of the Szczyrbskie Lake and in the Biała Liptowska Valley, gold-bearing sands from the beds of some streams were panned. By the 15th and 16th centuries, miners, called *hawiar* in the Podhale dialect, exploited low-grade ore deposits in the very harsh terrain of many regions of the Tatras. At that time, veins of ores found in the rocks of the crystalline block provided mainly copper containing small amounts of silver and traces of gold. Large-scale prospecting and mining also spread to the Polish part of the Tatras at that time, particularly the region of Ornak. Drifts in the sides of this mountain were dug from the direction of both the Kościeliska and the Starorobociańska Valleys. Mining was undertaken many times in this region, but was usually abandoned very quickly, as the yield did not cover the costs. News of this mining activity attracted adventurers from all over Europe in search of the legendary, immeasurable riches hidden deep in the heart of the Tatras. Other frequent visitors were collectors of therapeutic herbs and other natural medicinal substances, including various minerals, as well as lime-water and the bones of extinct animals, which could be found only in caves. Thus the first exploration of the Tatras was stimulated by material gain – the profit motive. In the second half of the 16th century, the Tatras were visited by the first explorers, followed by scientists interested in studying the aesthetic values of mountain nature. Until the end of the 17th century, the negative human impact on the Tatra nature was insignificant and meant that only small areas were permanently affected.

However, as time passed, the human pressure on the natural environment of the Tatras increased. Animal husbandry developing in the neighbouring Podtatrze region required more and more meadows and mountain pastures in Tatra clearings and above the tree-line. To increase the area of pastures, forests and dwarf mountain pine brushwood were felled. Hunting developed with periodic increases in poaching. More and more wood was cut in the Tatra forests for housing and the timber industry. In the 18th century, balms and medicinal oils of Europe-wide renown were distilled from the Swiss stone pine and dwarf mountain pine, while riverboats filled with fieldfares caught in great numbers in Orava sailed down the Wisła river all the way to Warsaw and Gdańsk. Towards the end of the 18th century, mining and smelting began to develop again in the Tatras. This time, it was iron ore, found mainly in the sedimentary rock of the *wierchy* and nappe units, that was mined and processed on a large scale. The burgeoning iron industry required huge amounts of charcoal, whose production often led to excessive, destructive felling of the Tatra forests. In less than a century, the more accessible forest stands of the lower sub-alpine belt were all felled to satisfy the needs of the iron works. The largest iron works from that time operated in Kuźnice Zakopiańskie. During their heyday in the mid-19th century, iron ore for their production processes was extracted from several mines located in the Western Tatras from the Kopa Magury to the Bobrowiec Mountains. Charcoal necessary for iron smelting and its further processing was produced mainly in the forests of the eastern part of the Tatras, in the Rybi Potok and Roztoka Valleys and many small nappe valleys. Consequently, the Kuźnice iron works had an adverse impact on a significant area of the Polish part of the Tatras. Towards the end of the 19th century, the damage to the lower sub-alpine forests of the Tatras was compounded by the felling of trees to serve the requirements of two paper mills in Kuźnice Zakopiańskie, and later the rapidly developing sawmills of Zakopane. This deforestation intensified the erosion of the bare Tatra slopes, and water-spates from them caused increasingly frequent floods, threatening the residents of the densely-populated valleys at the foot of the mountains.

Another important stage in the history of Tatra exploration began at the turn of the 19th century. At that time, the Tatra massif was more and more frequently visited by famous European scientists and travellers, including Robert Townson, an English naturalist, Baltazar Hacquet, a natural history professor of Lvov, François Beudant, a French geologist and Goran Wahlenber, a Swedish naturalist. Their travel and research accounts of the Tatras broadened the knowledge of the natural and ethnographic value of this mountain group among European scientists. Apart from various scientific observations, some of these works and other early 19th century publications also included early information about the dangers and damage to the Tatra nature being caused by excessive human activity. One of the first to raise this issue was the Polish geologist Stanisław Staszic, in his work entitled *O ziemiorodztwie Karpatow i innych gor i rownin Polski (On the Geology of the Carpathians and Other Polish Mountains and Lowlands)* published in 1815 in Warsaw.

"Gemse" – a hand-coloured figure from an unknown mid-19th century German-language publication, pasted into jointly bound copies of Kozica and Świstak of Maksymilian Nowicki (TPN archive)

In the early 19th century, the Tatra valleys and peaks came to be visited by increasing numbers of travellers and scientists, as well as artists – poets and painters – for whom the wild landscape of the Tatras and the people living and working there constituted a source of creative inspiration. The danger to the Tatra nature was noted more and more often. The first efforts to protect

The source of the Czarny Dunajec in the Kościeliska Valley. A lithograph by Emmanuel Kronbach, published around 1820

The Tatras on the geological map of the Carpathians by S. Staszic, published in 1815. The number 62 denotes goldmines, 66 – silver mines and 67 – iron ore mines

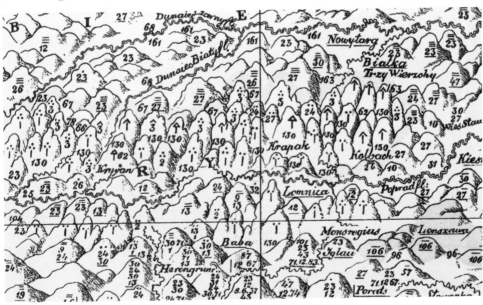

the animal species being thoughtlessly exterminated were made in the mid-19th century. Many years of efforts and endeavours by Polish scientists – Ludwik Zejszner, followed by Eugeniusz Janota and Maksymilian Nowicki – ended in an act prohibiting the hunting of chamois and marmots which was adopted by the National Parliament in Lvov on October 5, 1868. This act, published in 1869, represented the first law on animal species protection in the world.

Maciej Sieczka and Jędrzej Wala – the first rangers protecting Tatra chamois and alpine marmots. A photograph by A. Szubert, 1869 (TPN archive)

The year 1873 saw the establishment of the Tatra Society (*Towarzystwo Tatrzańskie*). Its purpose was to make the Tatras accessible to tourists, to organise scientific research and to protect Tatra nature. To this end, in 1875, the Society employed two rangers to safeguard the chamois. Several years later (1885), a lecture by a forester, Gustaw Lettner, entitled "*The Project to Save the Tatra and Particularly Zakopane Forests from their Threatened Destruction*" was printed in *Pamiętnik*, the Tatra Society journal. In 1888, the same periodical printed an article by Father Bogusław Królikowski (writing under the pseudonim of X. Wielkopolanin) entitled "*The Polish Tatras as the Monument to Adam Mickiewicz*". This was the first project for a national park in the Tatras, to be established following the example of the Yellowstone National Park of the US, the first national park in the world, founded in 1872. At the time, these efforts did not receive any broad support from Polish society, while the Tatra Society had no funds to buy forests and alpine pastures from their private owners.

The end of the 19th century witnessed the final collapse of the inefficient Tatra mining and metallurgy industry, and a reduction of poaching. However, new and increasing threats to the Tatra nature appeared, this time connected with the excessive development of tourism and its infrastructure: roads, trails, mountain lodges, railways and other extravagant attractions. This excessive taming of the mountains was opposed for many years by a group of scientists: naturalists and supporters of nature protection united in the Tatra Protection Branch of the Tatra Society, established in 1912. The efforts of this branch included lectures popularising the knowledge of the Tatra nature in the society, and the publication of posters aimed at protecting the most endangered mountain plant species. The main driving force behind this branch was its idealistic leader, Jan Gwalbert Pawlikowski, the author of many works on nature protection. Another active member was a forester, Stanisław Sokołowski, who published a project for the organisation of the Tatra National Park in a brochure entitled *Tatry jako park narodowy (The Tatras as a National Park)*. In 1924–1925, scientists from Poland and Czechoslovakia met twice to develop a joint proposal for a national park to cover the whole of the Tatras. In 1930s, the Polish State bought a part of the Tatras from its private owners. The year 1936 saw the establishment of the Organising Committee of the Tatra National Park, which by 1937 drafted a regulation of the Council of Ministers establishing a national park in the Tatras. A decree establishing a so-called Nature Park in a part of the Tatras was finally published in 1939, immediately before the outbreak of World War II, but it never came into force. The establishment of a national park in the Tatras had to wait until the end of the war. In 1947, an administrative unit of the State Forests called the Tatra National Park was created. The year 1948 saw the creation of the Pyszna strict reserve in the upper part of the Kościeliska Valley, and October 30, 1954 saw the publication of the first Regulation of the Council of Ministers establishing the Tatra National Park, which began its activities on January 1, 1955. The new Regulation of the Council of Ministers on the Tatra National Park of 1 April 2003 was drafted in accordance with the Nature Protection Act of 16 October 1991 and its revision of 2001. It came into effect in May 2003.

Thanks to these many years of efforts, the natural and cultural values of the Tatras have been preserved for future generations of aficionados and researchers of wild mountain nature. At the foot of the mountains, in the Podtatrze Region, the traditional culture of the highlanders – the original inhabitants of this area – has been kept alive, with its specific local dialect, folk-customs, architecture and traditional farming methods as applied in the past. The former sheep farming in the mountains was replaced in 1982 by what is referred to as "cultural shepherding" in selected Tatra clearings. What remains of the sheep farming are the shepherds' huts and wayside shrines preserved in the Tatra landscape, as well as the names of the surrounding valleys and peaks. Relics of other human activity in the Tatras are also protected inside the Park, e.g. the traces of past mining and iron-working.

Sheep grazing in Tatra clearings selected by scientists

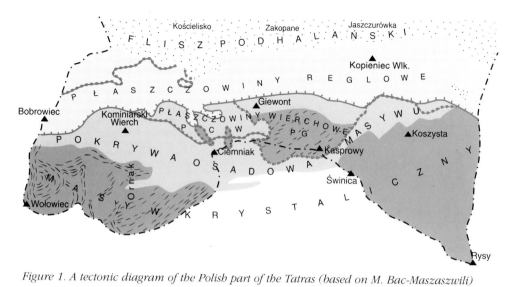

Figure 1. A tectonic diagram of the Polish part of the Tatras (based on M. Bac-Maszaszwili)

Tatra granite and the overlaying sedimentary rocks (red sandstone) in the vicinity of Żółta Turnia

II. Inanimate nature

Geological structure

The geological structure of the Tatras is typical for Alpine fold mountains. It comprises the following characteristic tectonic units: granitoid crystalline block and the folded and shifted sedimentary rocks of the *wierchy* and nappe units. The oldest metamorphic rocks were formed over 300 million years ago. In the Paleozoic era, towards the end of the Carboniferous period, a magma intrusion occurred which metamorphosed the surrounding older sedimentary rocks and solidified into a huge granitoid complex. The crystalline rocks created then (both metamorphic and magmatic) now make up the so-called crystalline block. In its border zone, the remains of postmagmatic solutions formed pegmatite veins containing large crystals of quartz, feldspar and mica. In the last period of the formation of this block, mineral veins crystallised in its cracks and fissures. These veins contain iron and copper sulphides with a small proportion of silver and were mined in the past.

The sedimentary rocks of the Tatras were formed mainly in the Mesozoic era. In changing geological conditions, the area of the present-day Tatras was either a sea (the Tethys ocean) in which various plants and animals lived and evolved, or dry land, on which processes of landform development and destruction took place. In the late Mesozoic era, some 100 million years ago, a series of orogenic processes, known as the Alpine orogenesis, deformed the original area of the Tatras. At that time, series of sedimentary strata from the Tethys ocean were folded as a result of the collision of two continental plates – the African and the Eurasian ones – pressing against each other. Horizontal pressure along the south-north axis shifted sediments from the south onto the land lying to the north. A body of rock shifted by folding-over is called a nappe. During this period, shallow sea sediments separated from the underlying rock were successively piled one on top of the other on the area of the Tatras. They form the Czerwone Wierchy nappe and the Giewont nappe. Today, together with the rocks forming the sedimentary cover of the crystalline block, they make up the *wierchy* units. During a later period, deep-sea sediments from the areas of Križna and Choč (present-day Slovakia) were torn off and shifted far to the north. These are the Križna and Choč nappes, which currently form the nappe units of the Tatras. The original Tatra massif folded in the late Cretaceous period and pushed above sea level was then strongly damaged by erosion processes.

In the early Tertiary period, in the Eocene epoch, the Tatra area subsided again. For the last time, it was covered by a shallow sea, in which conglomerates, limestone and dolomite were formed from single-celled organisms called foraminifers. Their shells formed calcareous rocks, most frequently numulitic limestones, which now constitute the natural border of the Tatra massif whose exposures can be seen when entering almost any valley on the

Typical glacial landforms in the granite part of the High Tatras

north side of the Tatras. The next important event in the formation of the Tatras occurred some 15 million years ago. At that time, a huge tectonic fault, which now separates the Tatras from the Liptov basin, developed in the south-eastern part of the Tatra massif. Along this fault, the south-eastern part of the Tatras was elevated by several kilometres. The lifting of the southern side of the massif caused the northerly sloping and a repeated folding and shifting of the sedimentary rocks and the nappes covering them. The traces of these past geological processes which have formed the Tatra massif are quite well preserved and are an interesting subject of study for geologists working on the tectonics of the Tatras.

The long and complicated history of the formation of the Tatra orogenesis has produced the richness and diversity of rocks found here. The dominant metamorphic rocks are the various types of crystalline shales, gneiss and amphibolites, currently found chiefly in the main ridge of the Western Tatras. Magmatic rocks (granodiorites and granites) are the material of which the highest Tatra peaks are made. The middle and northern parts of the Western Tatras as well as the northern part of the High Tatras are made up of a mosaic of sedimentary rocks. These are mainly limestones, dolomites, sandstones, shales and conglomerates of various ages.

Land relief

The complicated geological structure of the Tatras is reflected in their land relief. In the Pleistocene, glaciers transformed the gentle, dome-shaped forms dating back to the Tertiary period (Pliocene epoch) and their only surviving fragments can still be seen in the highest parts of the Czerwone Wierchy ridge.

The Pleistocene climate change, and in particular the cold cycles, have caused the permanent snow line in the Tatras to periodically descend to some 1,500–1,600 m a.s.l. (today that line lies at 2,300 m a.s.l.). As a result, above that line snow from one winter survived until the next. In the upper parts of the valleys it was gradually transformed into

The Dolina Mułowa Valley, a glacial cirque with its frontal moraine preserved

granular firn and then into ice. At that time, the Tatras had typical mountain glaciers, like the ones today seen in the Alps or other high mountains. The numerous, repeated local glaciations of the Tatra massif only ended some 9,000 years ago. During that period, a very characteristic glacial land relief developed in the Tatra mountains. Among its numerous and varied landforms, the most characteristic are the steep rock walls, sharp ridges, hanging valleys, vertical series of cirques, glacial troughs, the profiles of former river valleys (V-shaped) were transformed into glaciated valleys (U-shaped), rock polishing and glacial grooves as well as various types of moraines – lateral, basal, terminal – which now fill the bottoms of most valleys. All of these and some additional glacial forms are still very visible in the relief of the Tatras. Glaciers caused a stronger transformation of the relief of the High Tatras, which were several hundred metres higher than the Western Tatras. During the peak of the glaciation, glaciers filling the High Tatra valleys flowed down to the northern edge of these mountains, with the longest glacier filling the Białka Valley stretching for almost 20 km. In the Western Tatras, the glaciers were much shorter and only reached to the middle of the valleys. In this part of the Tatras, the most important landforms are the former postglacial cirques – the Litworowa and Mułowa Valleys, with terminal moraine surviving in the latter.

Since the melting of the glaciers, the relief of the Tatras has been undergoing further transformations. At present, the most important land forming processes are: gravitational degeneration (breaking off, rockfalls, slides), the effects of flowing water and rainwater, the wind, snow and avalanches. Karst processes play a major role in areas built of carbonate rocks. Land relief is clearly connected with the resilience of the ground, which in turn depends on its geological structure. In weaker parts, rock walls are bisected by gullies at the feet of which scree cones form. Areas built of rocks more resistant to weathering and erosion usually become convex forms as peaks, pinnacles, ridges and lone rocks. Areas built of rocks susceptible to erosion, as well as the zones of faults and tectonic cracks develop into concave forms – passes, gullies and valleys. In the streams, rock resistant to the action of water forms ledges and waterfalls, while hollows and eversion hollows are created in places susceptible to erosion. The Tatras sometimes give us an opportunity to

Figure 2. A diagram of glacier distribution during the last glaciation in the Polish part of the Tatras (based on M. Bac-Maszaszwili)

Contemporary landforming processes – a mud and rubble slide near Ornak, June 1993

observe very violent present-day land forming processes. These include snow and rock avalanches, rockfalls, as well as mud and rubble slides. These processes are usually initiated by heavy rainfall or snowfall.

Caves

Areas built mainly of calcareous rocks (mainly limestone and dolomite) feature interesting karst relief (the name comes from the geographic area of Karst located at the border of Italy and Slovenia). It consists of various surface and underground forms created by complex physical and chemical processes during which the weakly soluble carbonate rocks are dissolved by water which has picked up carbon dioxide, usually from the humus part of the soil. Karst areas are dominated by picturesque limestone massifs or outcroppings with clint and gryke limestone pavements cut in them. One can also find characteristic depressions, called sinkholes, usually filled with snow until late summer. The rock surfaces are covered with small-scale forms of relief, most noticeably karst grooves of various shapes and sizes as well as cracks through which water penetrates underground and erodes subterranean voids. The same role is also played by the aforementioned sinkholes. Underground corridors that a man can enter are called caves. Their openings sometimes appear as black holes in rock faces, but usually are hidden behind rock corners or in other, less visible places.

In the Tatras, karst landforms are seen mainly in the *wierchy* part of the Western Tatras, in the vicinity of the Kominiarski Wierch, Czerwone Wierchy and Giewont peaks, where limestone dominates. This location means that the relief that develops is karst scenery characteristic of high mountains. Interesting forms of karst relief are accessible to the

*High mountain karst
in the Czerwone Wierchy massif*

The outflow from under Pisana

tourists in Wąwóz Krakow, a part of the Kościeliska Valley. This karst canyon also features a number of caves, which are the most interesting underground natural attraction in areas built of carbonate rocks.

The process of cave formation is very long and complex. It started in the Tertiary period, after the Tatra massif emerged from the Tethys ocean, and is still in progress. The oldest, pre-Eocene karst forms have already been destroyed by the progressing erosion of the limestone massifs. Underground karst forms created in subsequent geological periods have usually been transformed many times by the underground flow of water and have survived in the resulting shape until today. Close to valley bottoms, one usually finds caves which are still being intensively enlarged by underground flows of water. They include the Wodna Cave near Pisana, located close to the exit of Wąwóz Kraków, from the mouth of which the Kościeliski Stream flows to the surface. Several hundred meters upstream, the stream disappears in a zone of swallow holes (ponors) feeding underground cracks not yet accessible to man.

Naturalists, however, are mainly interested in old, extensive cave systems formed several hundred thousand years ago, which still carry water from the surface of karst areas to underground water courses. In these caves, one can observe chambers, corridors and systems of other forms bearing witness to the long period of formation and evolution of

Dripstone cover in the Szczelina Chochołowska Cave

these underground water routes. In addition to this information, the sediments filling these caves also tell us about the climate changes in the Tatras in the previous epoch (paleoclimate) or animals previously inhabiting this region (paleozoology). Cave sediments are divided into: clastic (alluvial deposits), organic (animal bones) and chemical (dripstone). All these types of sediment are of great interest to scientists, while chemical sediments also fascinate tourists and cave explorers. Unfortunately, the dripstone forms of Tatra caves are very sparse. The climate prevailing in these mountains was not favourable to their formation, and the forms that did develop during the warm interglacial periods were destroyed by huge underground flows of water from glaciers melting after successive glaciations.

Conversely, cave sediments have survived undamaged due to the special microclimate of caves. The deeper parts of larger caves have constant temperatures approaching the

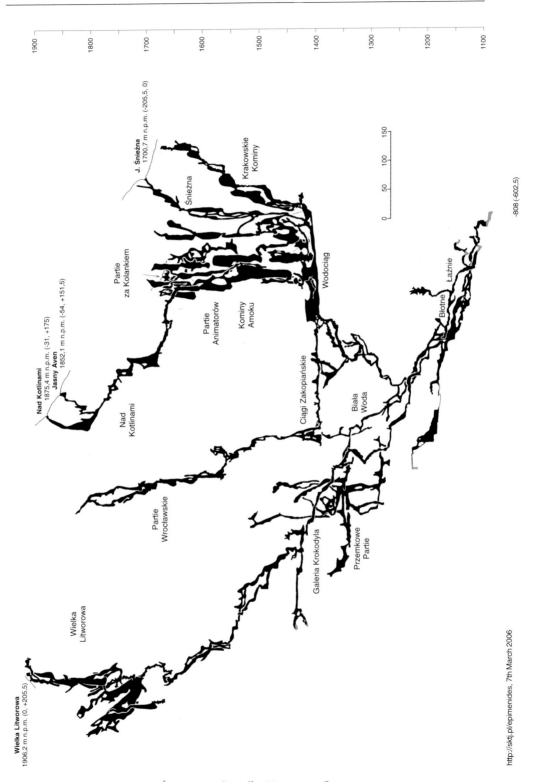

Figure 3. A diagram of Wielka Śnieżna and Wielka Litworowa Caves

annual average temperature on the surface and a high humidity of almost 100%. In some Tatra caves, the climate conditions enable ice forms to develop and survive throughout the year. These so-called ice caves are, however, very rare. Significant quantities of ice survive throughout the year only in a dozen or so caves, of which the best known one is the Lodowa Cave in Ciemniak. Regardless of the extremely difficult living conditions, various organisms inhabit the caves. Many moss species grow close to the cave mouths, but as one goes deeper, they give way to fungi and bacteria. Caves are also the home to many animal species. These are divided into three groups. The first are trogloxenes and stygoxenes – animals accidentally found in caves. These include bats and some insects. Troglophiles and stygophiles are animals living both on the surface and in caves: they include some spiders and beetles. The typical inhabitants of caves are called troglobionts and stygobionts. These animals display many adaptations to underground life. A representative of this group is the crustacean *Niphargus tatriensis*. The variety of natural phenomena seen in caves is the main reason for their exceptional scientific and educational value.

For many years, the caves in the Tatras have been explored and visited by many people. So far, 700 caves with the total length of accessible passages exceeding 120 km have been explored in the Polish part of the Tatras. The majority are small, less than 10 m long. Only slightly more than 60 measure more than 100 m in length, while only 16 are longer than 1 km. The largest cave is the five-mouth connected system of the Wielka Śnieżna and Wielka Litworowa Caves, whose length exceeds 22,000 m and a vertical range of 824 m. The next longest are the systems of the Wysoka – Za Siedmioma Progami Cave (11,660 m) and Miętusia Cave (10,500 m). The deepest caves, after Wielka Śnieżna, are Śnieżna Studnia (763 m) and Bańdzioch Kominiarski (562 m). The largest Tatra caves are very difficult to access and their exploration requires climbing expertise. However, 6 caves in the Tatra National Park are accessible to tourists: Mroźna, Mylna, Obłaskowa, Raptawicka and Smocza Jama in the Kościeliska Valley as well as Dziura in the Dolina ku Dziurze Valley. The Mroźna Cave is the only show cave with electric lighting and guided tours.

Climate

The climate of the Tatras has the features of a high mountain climate of the temperate zone. It is dominated by the flow of polar sea air-masses from the west. Sometimes, particularly in winter, this area receives polar continental air-masses flowing from the east and north-east. Due to the high elevation above sea level, the Tatras have climatic zones arranged in belts. The greater the elevation, the lower the average annual air temperature, ranging from 6°C to approximately -4°C on the highest peaks. Consequently, the higher one goes, the shorter the vegetative season becomes.

The Tatra climate is also characterised by highly variable weather, rapid pressure changes, temperature inversions, high relative air humidity and the highest annual precipitation in Poland, ranging from some 1,200 mm at the base to approximately 2,000 mm on Kasprowy Wierch. At the base of the Tatras, rain is the dominant form of precipitation, whereas higher up, the majority of precipitation is in the form of snow. As the altitude rises, the quantity of horizontal precipitation, i.e. water vapour condensating in the form of hoarfrost, for example, increases. Thunderstorms with their dangerous atmospheric discharges are also much more frequent in the mountains than in the lowlands. The Tatra peaks are particularly hazardous during thunderstorms. The most dangerous one is Giewont, where many people have been killed by lightning. The duration of snow cover also depends on

Landscape with melting snow

During an inversion, clouds tightly cover Tatra peaks

the altitude. At the foot of the Tatras, continuous snow cover lasts from November to April, and in the fell band – from October to June. Snow depth varies, depending mainly on the local orographic conditions. The greatest snow depth recorded on the summit of Kasprowy Wierch exceeded 350 cm, but snow can be even deeper in concave landforms. On the other hand, snow is frequently blown off ridges and open slopes even during very snowy winters. During that season, the wind often forms cornices on ridges, which pose a danger to tourists. Another hazard to winter visitors to Tatras is posed by snow avalanches, which, after very heavy snowfalls, can spontaneously slide down slopes above the tree-line. Low air temperatures, which can occur at any time of the year, can cause ice to form on trails, chains and ladder rungs. Peculiarities of the Tatra climate include relatively frequent temperature inversions, and a local foehn wind called *halny*. This is a strong, dry, warm wind from the south or south-west. It is most frequent in spring and autumn, but can also come in other seasons of the year. During the *halny* wind, a characteristic bank of clouds is visible. Gusts of wind often exceed 50 m/s, but stronger gusts have been recorded. During the *halny* wind of 6 May 1968, which had tragic consequences for Tatra forest stands, gusts of wind reached 80 m/s (ca. 290 km/h). Rapid pressure and temperature changes can even pose a danger to people with circulatory disorders.

The Sucha Woda Stream bed

Waters

The Tatra Mountains lie in the catchment basins of the Black and the Baltic Seas, but the entire area of the Tatra National Park belongs to the Baltic Sea catchment area. The European watershed runs through the Tatras, at first along the side ridge from the Molkówka Clearing to Wołowiec, and then along the main ridge from Wołowiec to Cubryna. Because of their abundant precipitation, the Tatras are well-supplied with water. Most of it flows away in the warm half of the year, when the precipitation is the greatest and at the same time the snow melts. In winter, streams carry little water. Water features in the Polish part of the Tatras have a belt layout caused by the geological structure of the land. For this reason, three hydrological regions are distinguished: the southern crystalline region, the middle karst one and the northern dolomite and shale region.

The southern region, where the bedrock is crystalline (granitoids and metamorphic rocks), is characterised by a permanent, relatively dense river network, numerous springs with small flows, low water retentiveness of the ground and large changes in water levels depending on the season and the precipitation level. The majority of Tatra lakes and tarns are found in this part of the Tatras.

The middle region, where the bedrock is carbonate and thus subject to karst phenomena, is characterised by a seasonal river network, underground streams and a high water retentiveness of the ground. The characteristic feature of this region is the lateral flow of water between catchments, always in a westerly direction. For example, the water from

Zielony Staw and Kurtkowiec Tarns in the Stawów Gąsienicowych Valley

the Czerwone Wierchy massif surfaces at the Lodowe Spring in the Kościeliska Valley. In the southern part of the karst area, streams often lose water, which then flows underground. Such stream beds carrying no water are referred to as *suche wody* – dry streams. On the other hand, the northern border of this area has many copious karst (rising) springs. The largest ones are: Wywierzysko Olczyskie, Wywierzysko Bystrej, Wywierzysko Chochołowskie and the Lodowe Spring. Each one of them produces several hundred litres of water per second. The flow of streams fed by these springs is fairly even throughout the year. These streams also have a constant temperature, close to the average annual air temperature. This is why, in the past, iron works and forges were located on the banks of streams fed by karst springs.

The northern region, where the bedrock consists of dolomites and shales, is characterised by a permanent river network with a relatively even flow throughout the year.

One of the landscape attractions of the Tatras are numerous postglacial lakes, of which the smaller ones are called tarns (Polish *staw*). The Polish Tatras boast over a hundred of such natural, picturesque bodies of standing water. The largest one of them is called Morskie Oko (34.5 ha) and the deepest is Wielki Staw Polski (79.3 m). Tatra lakes located above the tree-line have a sparse biological life (oligotrophic lakes) and unusually clear water. The few shallow, peaty lakes in the forest belt are characterised by a rich biological life (dystrophic lakes). Such lakes include Toporowe Stawy in the Brzeziny region and Smreczyński Staw in the Kościeliska Valley.

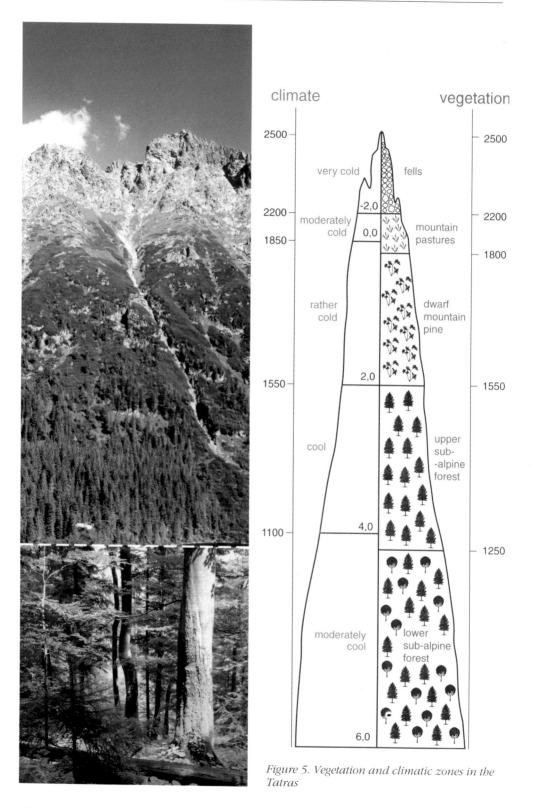

climate   vegetation

2500 —

very cold   fells

                -2,0
2200 —   — 2200
           moderately
             cold   0,0
1850 —   mountain
                                 pastures   — 1800

           rather
             cold   dwarf
                                 mountain
                                 pine

                      2,0
1550 —   — 1550

           cool   upper
                                 sub-
                                 -alpine
                                 forest

                      4,0
1100 —   — 1250

                                 lower
           moderately   sub-alpine
             cool   forest

                      6,0

Figure 5. Vegetation and climatic zones in the Tatras

III. Flora and fauna

The high diversification of the abiotic environment of the Tatras, and in particular the varied geological structure, habitat conditions, relief, water relationships and climatic conditions contribute to the development of a plant cover clearly different from that of other Polish regions. The Tatra vegetation is also distinguished by its great richness and variety of forms, which are obvious to all visitors to this area. The special features of Tatra vegetation have been the reason why a separate unit – the Tatry district – has been distinguished in the geobotanical classification of the Polish Carpathians.

The most visible feature of the Tatra vegetation is its belt arrangement. During a one day climb from the foot of the Tatras to their highest peaks, one can observe plant communities ranging from those of the forest belt to communities of the fell belt, just below the permanent snow line. With the increase of altitude above sea level, the climate becomes more severe (lower temperatures, greater precipitation and shorter vegetative season), gradually changing whole plant formations making up the particular belts. The high-growing forests become more sparse, with dwarfed trees, and then, above the tree-line, are replaced by a mountain dwarf pine brushwood. Higher still, there are only alpine grasslands in the mountain pasture belt. In the highest belt of fells, only small tufts of plants grow on the rocky precipices. These are usually plants well adapted to growing in extremely difficult conditions: tufts of grass, plants forming cushions, viviparous plants, low row shrubs and lichens forming a mosaic of different coloured patches on rocks.

Within the curve of the Carpathians, the Tatras are the main area where a mountain vegetation of exceptional diversity occurs. Over 1,000 species of vascular plants have been counted here and represent almost 43% of all vascular plant species found in Poland. This number includes over 400 species of mountain plants, of which some 200 grow only in the Tatras. Very many – over 100 species of plants found in the Tatras – are subject to species protection in Poland. Among trees and bushes, these include the Swiss pine *Pinus cembra*, *Pinus rhaetica*, the dwarf mountain pine *Pinus mugo*, the yew *Taxus baccata*, which has been almost exterminated and is now very rare, and the daphne *Daphne mezereum*. Groups of protected plants abundant in the Tatras include the orchid family – 27 species, gentians – 11 species, lycopods – 7 species and anemones – 3 species. 14 taxa subject to species protection in Poland are found only in the Tatras. These include *Chamaeorchis alpina*, *Dianthus glacialis*, the stemless gentian *Gentiana clusii*, *Gentiana frigida*, the snow gentian *Gentiana nivalis*, *Gentianella lutescens*, *Gentianella tenella*, *Gymnadenia odoratissima*, the tussock-grass *Poa granitica* and *Pulsatilla slavica*. Species protected by law in Poland also include plants symbolic for the region: the edelweiss *Leontopodium alpinum*, efforts to protect which begun as early as in the second half of the 19th century, and the Turk's cap lily *Lilium martagon*.

Dark-winged orchid

Stemless gentian

Club-moss

Anemone

Turk's cap lily

The floral autonomy of the Tatras is also evidenced by the occurrence of almost 90 plant taxa (species, subspecies and varieties) considered to be endemic or sub-endemic to the Tatras, to the Eastern Carpathians, Western Carpathians or the Carpathians as a whole. Species endemic to the Tatras currently include: tussock-grasses *Poa granitica* and *P. nobilis*, the scurvy grass *Cochlearia tatrae* (returned to the list) and 16 taxa of a lower order. Species endemic to Western Carpathians, whose main centre of distribution lies in the Tatras include: *Saxifraga wahlenbergii* and the larkspur *Delphinium oxysepalum,* which at the same time constitute paleoendemic species. Other species endemic or sub-endemic to the Western Carpathian which are frequently found in the Tatras are: *Soldanella carpatica*, the fescue *Festuca tatrae, Cerastium tatrae*, the grass pink *Diantus plumarius subsp. praecox,* and the saffron *Crocus scepusiensis.* Species endemic to the whole Carpathians and found in the Tatras include: the fescue *Festuca carpatica*, the willow *Salix kitaibeliana*, the thyme *Thymus pulcherrimus*, the crazy weed *Oxytropis carpatica* and *Erigeron hungaricus*. Species sub-endemic to the whole Carpathians occurring in the Tatras include: *Cardaminopsis neglecta*, the toothwort *Dentaria glandulosa*, the comfrey *Symphytum cordatum, Leucanthemum waldsteinii* and the fescue *Festuca versicolor.*

Plants characteristic for the Tatras also include relic species, i.e. plants which formed an element of the plant cover of the Tatras in the past. Two paleoendemic species are classified among the oldest relic species, dating back to the Pliocene epoch of the Tertiary period: *Saxifraga wahlenbergii* and the larkspur *Delphinium oxysepalum.* During the warm interglacial periods of the Pleistocene, species from other mountain areas of the Central and Eastern Europe reached the Tatras. Such European species include primroses *Primula auricula* and *P. minima, Homogyne alpina* and the buttercup *Ranunculus alpestris*. The following species have probably reached the Tatras from the Mediterranean region: the blue-bell *Campanula alpina, Saxifraga caesia* and the whitlow-wort *Draba aizoides*, while the Northern Europe was the source of the willow *Salix herbacea* and the mountain avens *Dryas octopetala*. The edelweiss *Leontopodium alpinum* and the gentian *Gentiana frigida* may have travelled to the Tatras all the way from Asia, whereas the American continent was the original home of *Saxifraga hieraciifolia* and the goldenrod *Solidago virgaurea.*

Another important feature bearing witness to the autonomy of the Tatra plant cover is the occurrence of many endemic associations characteristic for these mountains. Such endemic Tatra associations include *Oreochloetum distichae subnivale*, the association of the fescue *Festuco versicoloris-Seslerietum tatrae* and of the fescue with the bent grass *Festuco versicoloris-*

Agrostietum alpinae, as well as *Saxifragetum wahlenbergii*. Some other plant associations have been found, apart from the Tatras, only in the adjoining mountain ranges.

The world of lower plants, less obvious to the tourists, is also rich and varied. In the Tatras, almost 3,000 species of mosses, liverworts, algae, lichens, large-bodied fungi, parasitic fungi and slime moulds (Myxomycetes) are found in different habitats. The lower plants also exhibit changes in distribution related to the altitude. However, whereas the number of vascular plant species clearly decreases with an increase in altitude, the number of species of mosses, liverworts and lichens actually increases. These plants are probably better adapted to life in extreme alpine conditions. Among the lower plants there are many interesting mountain species found only in the Tatras. Some of them have turned out to be species new to the Polish flora, but some have also been new to science. Of the numerous group of lichens, 26 species are subject to species protection in Poland.

The animal world of the Tatras is no less interesting and is extremely varied. Over 8,000 animal species have been found in the Tatras so far, but the overwhelming majority of them are invertebrates, usually unnoticed by tourists. One of the more numerous and very characteristic groups of Tatra animals are birds. Only a little over 100 species of breeding birds build nests in the Tatras. Several dozen other species have been observed here during their spring and autumn migrations. Usually those are fresh-water birds, but even some typical sea-birds have been seen very infrequently. Many other bird species, very rare in Poland, have occasionally been seen in the Tatras. In recent decades these included the booted eagle *Hieraaetus pennatus*, the hawk owl *Surnia ulula*, the scops owl *Otus scops*, the pygmy owl *Glaucidium passerinum*, and even, for the first time in Poland, three specimens of the alpine swift *Apus melba* have been observed here. The total number of birds in the Tatras is estimated at 55,000 pairs, of which chaffinches *Fringilla coelebs* and robins *Erithacus rubecula* represent over 30%. The Tatras are home to seven species of amphibians: the common newt *Triturus vulgaris*, the Carpathian newt *T. montandonii* and the spotted salamander *Salamandra salamandra*, the yellow-bellied toad *Bombina variegata*, the common toad *Bufo bufo* and the common grass frog *Rana temporaria* as well as three species of reptiles: the scaly lizard *Lacerta vivipara*, the common northern viper *Vipera berus* and the grass snake *Natrix natrix*. Only some Tatra tarns and streams are inhabited by six fish species. The native species are: the salmon trout *Salmo trutta*, *Cottus poecilopus*, the brook minnow *Phoxinus phoxinus* and the grayling *Thymallus thymallus*, whereas humans introduced the brook trout *Salvelinus fontinalis* and the rainbow trout *Salmo gairdneri*. Over 50 species of mammals constitute a relatively

Scurvy grass

Clematis

Larkspur

Carpathian snowbells

Primrose

Trentepohlia joithos algae growing on granites, the so-called violet stone

numerous and very characteristic group of Tatra animals. The most numerous are rodents – 18 species, followed by bats (17 species), predators (12 species) and insectivorous mammals (7 species).

Almost 230 species of animals living in the Tatras are subject to species protection in Poland. Among those, the most numerous are birds – 99 species of breeding birds, insects – 40 species, and mammals – 35 species.

The animal world in the Tatras changes along with the changes in habitats and the vegetation. In this case, the vertical differentiation is less pronounced, though just as in the plant kingdom, the higher one goes, the fewer animals one finds. In the Tatras, many animals find their upper range-limit. Lower sub-alpine forests do not differ from other regions of Poland in terms of the diversity of animals living there.

Above these forest, one usually finds only alpine species and a few of those also found lower down. The specific conditions of the mountain climate mean that the animals living here, particularly insects, display many adaptations to life in severe alpine conditions. Such adaptations include a reduction in the number of generations compared to related lowland species, ovoviparousness as observed among some species of beetles, the scaly lizard and the common northern viper, and finally melanism, or a darker colouration connected with the lower temperature and increased humidity. Many insect species found in the mountains are very hairy to retain warmth better. Another insect adaptation is the loss of the ability to fly and akinesis, which means that an alarmed insect does not run away but becomes motionless and falls from the plant to the ground. Very many species living in the highest parts of the Tatras are diurnal, even though related species are nocturnal animals. One of the methods for surviving the severe climatic conditions is winter hibernation, characteristic for marmots, bats and some other animals.

The animals found in the Tatras can be divided into three groups. The first consists of species, usually insects, which appear at various elevations only in the summer and never breed in the Tatras.

The second group are animals permanently living in the Tatras, but also found outside these mountains. This group includes the majority of Tatra animals, and among them: the brown bear *Ursus arctos*, the lynx *Lynx lynx*, the wolf *Canis lupus*, the fox *Vulpes vulpes*, the red deer *Cervus elaphus*, the roe deer *Capreolus capreolus* and the otter *Lutra lutra*. Birds belonging to this group include: the European nutcracker *Nucifraga caryocatactes*, large forest gallinaceous birds: the black grouse *Tetrao tetrix*, the hazel grouse *Tetrastes bonasia* and the woodgrouse *Tetrao urogallus*, and among birds of pray: the golden eagle *Aquila chrysaetos,* the kestrel *Falco tinnunculus*, the peregrine falcon *Falco peregrinus* and the eagle owl *Bubo bubo.*

However, what makes the Tatra fauna special are those animals which are only found here. These include the chamois *Rupicapra rupicapra tatrica*, the alpine marmot *Marmota marmota latirostris*, the snow vole *Microtus nivalis mirhanreini* and the Tatra pine

A bear in the lower sub-alpine forest

Apollo butterfly

Roe deer

Common viper

Lynx

Eurasian nutcracker

Wolf

Lower sub-alpine
Carpathian beechwood.

vole *Pitymys tatricus* which is endemic to the Western Carpathians. Birds belonging to this group are: the alpine accentor *Prunella collaris* and the water pipit *Anthus spinoletta* as well as the wallcreeper *Tichodroma muraria* found outside the Tatras only in the Pieniny Mountains.

Many endemic and relic species are found among invertebrates inhabiting the Tatras at present: nematodes, water crustaceans, snails, spiders, harvestmen, collembolans and insects. The best known are beetles from the ground beetle family: *Nebrica tatrica* and *Carabus transsylvanicus*, ringlet butterflies *Erebia pronoe* and *E. pharte* found only in the Western Tatras and the apollo butterfly *Parnassius apollo*, exceedingly rare nowadays.

The sub-alpine forest belt

In the sub-alpine region, forests measure 12,800 ha in area and are the dominant plant formation of the upper and lower sub-alpine belt. In addition, this region also includes forest clearings and associations of rock plants.

The lower sub-alpine forest spreads from the foot of the Tatras to an elevation of 1,200–1,250 m a.s.l. The climatic conditions prevailing here are characteristic of the moderately cool climate belt, in which the average annual temperature is about 4°C and the annual precipitation reaches 1,400 mm. This belt, just as the other climatic belts of Tatras, features a large annual temperature amplitude exceeding 50°C and more rain than snow. Winter lasts some 130 days in a year here and, on the average, lying snow remains for 140 days.

In the lower sub-alpine forest, several plant associations are found depending on the local habitat conditions. In the past, this vegetation belt on the northern side of the Tatras was dominated by mixed forests of the fir *Abies alba* and the beech *Fagus sylvatica* with some proportion of sycamore *Acer pseudoplatanus* and on some soils also the spruce *Picea abies* as well as isolated yews *Taxus baccata*. These forests were significantly damaged in past centuries by the excessive felling of wood for the requirements of mining, smelting and the paper industry. They have survived until the present in a good condition only in the Zakopane sub-alpine forest region, in the Białego, Ku Dziurze, Spadowca, Strążyska and Za Bramką Valeys as well as on Samkowa Czuba and Grześkówki. These small forest areas surviving to the present day belong to the leading association of the lower sub-alpine forest, called the Carpathian beech wood *Dentario glandulosae-Fagetum*.

This association grows on soils with a high calcium carbonate content – rich brown and calcareous soils. The tree layer is dominated by beech, but firs sometimes also represent a major proportion. Sycamores and spruces are also present and yews are sporadically found. The shrub layer in the Carpathian beech wood is poorly developed. Of the more interesting species found in it, there is the daphne *Daphne mezereum*, a legally protected shrub that blooms in early spring, the goat willow *Salix caprea* and *Salix silesiaca*. In some locations, one can find the whitebeam *Sorbus aria* which in Poland grows only in the Tatra and Pieniny Mountains, as well as the fly honeysuckle *Lonicera xylosteum*, the black honeysuckle *Lonicera nigra*, the elder *Sambucus nigra* and the red elder *Sambucus racemosa*. The undergrowth includes the following plants characteristic for the Carpathian beech wood: a species endemic to the whole Carpathians – the toothwort *Dentaria glandulosa*, other toothworts: *D. bulbifera* and *D. enneaphyllos*, the violet *Viola reichenbachiana*, the yellow archangel *Galeobdolon luteum*, the white ginger *Asarum europaeum*, hollyferns

Daphne

Toothwort

Anemone

Lady's slipper

Spring gentian

Polystichum braunii, P. aculeatum and the cress *Cardamine trifolia*, very numerous in the Tatra beech woods. We can also find species that grow in beech woods all over Poland, like the herb paris *Paris quadrifolia*, the wood sorrel *Oxalis acetosella*, the wood anemone *Anemone nemorosa*, as well as the following protected species: the yellow ladies' slipper *Cypripedium calceolus*, the spring gentian *Gentiana verna* and the Turk's cap lily *Lilium martagon*. Among the plants characteristic for the Carpathian beech woods, the rarest in the Tatras are the comfrey *Symphytum cordatum* and the garlic *Allium ursinum*.

Apart from the Carpathian beech wood, there are two other forest associations found in the lower sub-alpine forest. An important one is the fir-spruce coniferous forest *Abieti-Piceetum montanum*, usually growing in poor habitats on granite bedrock. The forest stand is usually composed of two tree species: the fir and the spruce. In many places, the fir-spruce coniferous forests are of a secondary nature and have developed where former fir habitats and poor beech woods were planted with spruce. A significant area (over 960 ha) of the lower sub-alpine parts of the High Tatras is occupied by so-called lower sub-alpine moraine spruce woods, whose habitat has developed on the crystalline formations of postglacial moraines. This type of a mountain coniferous forest habitat is characteristic of the Tatras.

Heavy, rich soils, but poorer than those in the Carpathian beech woods, are usually covered by swathes of the rich fir forest *Galio-Abietetum*. Here the forest stand is predominantly composed of firs, with only a small proportion of spruces. Although many plant species characteristic of rich forests are found in the undergrowth, coniferous forest plant species start to predominate here. This latter group includes the wintergreen *Moneces uniflora*, the wavy hair grass *Deschampsia flexuosa*, the common buckler fern *Dryopteris dilatata*, the scented fern *D. expansa*, *Homogyne alpina* and the bilberry *Vaccinium myrtillus*.

Along streams, plant associations of the alderwood *Alnetum incanae* penetrate into the lower sub-alpine forest. This is a typical riverside carr of mountain areas growing on alluvial or brown soils. It is found in the lower sections of large Tatra valleys, like the Chochołowska, Kościeliska, Suchej Wody Valleys and by the Białka river. The forest stands here are dominated by the grey alder *Alnus incana* with a small proportion of the spruce *Picea alba*, the brittle willow *Salix fragilis* and sometimes also the European ash *Fraxinus excelsior* and the sycamore *Acer pseudoplatanus*. Among undergrowth plants, the species distinguishing this association are the touch-me-not *Impatiens nolitangere*, *Petasites kablikianus*, *Geranium robertianum*, *G. phaeum*, *Melandrium rubrum*, the buttercup *Ranunculus lanuginosus*, the stinging nettle *Urtica dioica*, the wild strawberry *Fragaria vesca* and the willow herb *Epilobium mantanum*.

A lower sub-alpine spruce forest on a moraine

Other forest associations of the lower sub-alpine forest occupy relatively small areas. They include the bog alder wood association *Caltho-Alnetum* growing on boggy and marshy areas, e.g. in the Zazadnia region and at the mouth of the Filipki Valley, as well as the Carpathian sycamore wood *Sorbo-Aceretum* growing on steep, often precipitous sides of limestone gullies and canyons. The latter can be observed in the lower part of the Kościeliska Valley.

Limestone and dolomite outcrops in the lower sub-alpine forest are sometimes over-grown by relic pine forests *Vario-Pinetum*. The forest stand here consists of low and

Gentian (Gentiana praecox)   *Flowering bilberry*

twisted specimens of the Scottish pine *Pinus sylvestris*. This tree is often accompanied by the whitebeam *Sorbus aria*, while the shrub layer includes the cotoneaster *Cotoneaster integerrima* and junipers *Juniperus communis*. The undergrowth is dominated by thermophilous species, which include the Lily of the Valley *Convallaria majalis*, Salomon's Seal *Polygonatum multiflorum*, *Sesleria tatrae*, the reed grass *Calamagrostis varia* and rare relic species like the common bearberry *Arctostaphylos uva-ursi* and the anemone *Pulsatilla slavica*.

There are limestone and dolomite outcrops in all valleys within the lower sub-alpine forest. They are overgrown by plants belonging to the pioneer association of the sedge and fescue *Carici-Festucetum tatrae*. This association includes florally rich tall grasslands on carbonate rocks and stabilised scree, where the topography prevents or strongly inhibits the development of forest vegetation. It is made up mainly of the Tatra sub-species of the evergreen sedge *Carex sempervirens ssp. tatrorum* and the fescue *Festuca tatrae*. It also includes limestone-loving plants like the pink *Dianthus praecox*, the sengreen *Sempervivum soboliferum ssp. preissianum*, the scabius *Knautia kitaibelii*, the thistle *Carduus glaucus*, the hawkweed *Hieracium villosum* and the dwarf alpine onion *Allium montanum*. On carbonate rock walls, one can also see single plants or groups of well-known, characteristic Tatra plants, including the primrose *Primula auricula*, the edelweiss *Leontopodium alpinum*, the stemless gentian *Gentiana clusii*, the alpine aster *Aster alpinus* and the saxifrage *Saxifraga aizoon*. Together with other plants, they make up one of the most species-rich plant associations in the Tatras.

Scottish pine

The upper sub-alpine forest grows between the altitudes of 1,250 and 1,550 m a.s.l. The climatic conditions here are characteristic for the cool climate belt, in which the annual average temperature is around 2°C and annual precipitation reaches 1,600 mm. This belt features more snow than rain. Winter lasts for some 155 days in the year here and the snow remains on the ground for an average of 180 days.

The more severe climate of this belt restricts the number of plant associations growing here. These changes are most obvious in the forest, dominated by spruces. As one climbs higher and higher above sea level, the dense, high-growing forest gradually becomes dwarfed and sparse, so that close to the tree-line only clusters of dwarf trees grow.

Plant associations dominating in the upper sub-alpine forest are the Western-Carpathian upper sub-alpine fir forest growing on a crystalline bedrock – *Plagiothecio-Piceetum tatricum* and a florally richer upper sub-alpine fir forest growing on a carbonate baserock – *Polysticho-Piceetum tatricum*. The forest stands of upper sub-alpine coniferous forests are made up of the Norway spruce *Picea abies*, sometimes with a small proportion of mountain ash *Sorbus aucuparia var. glabrata*. In the lower parts, one can find single sycamores *Acer pseudoplatanus*. At the tree-line, the Swiss stone pine *Pinus cembra* appears and forms the relic Swiss pine coniferous forest *Cembro-Piceetum*.

Acidophilous Western Carpathian upper sub-alpine spruce forests growing on a crystalline bedrock have a sparse undergrowth layer which includes several species endemic to the Carpathians, like the wood rush *Luzula luzulina* and *Soldanella carpatica*. Other undergrowth plants include the milkweed gentian *Gentiana asclepiadea*, the fir club-moss *Huperzia selago*, the stiff club-moss *Lycopodium annotinum*, the scented fern *Dryopteris expansa,* the bilberry *Vaccinium myrtillus* and the red bilberry *V. vitis-idaea*.

Upper sub-alpine spruce forests growing on a carbonate bedrock are characterised by a rich undergrowth, in which, apart from the plants found in acidofilous spruce forests, one can also find species characteristic for this association: the hollyfern *Polystychum lonchitis, Pirola uniflora* and the moss *Mnium spinosum*. Other species observed here are as follows: the toothwort *Dentaria glandulosa*, the saxifrage *Chrysosplenium alternifolium*, the valerian *Valeriana tripteris*, the violet *Viola biflora, Asplenium viridae* and the yellow archangel *Galeodbolon luteum*.

A biogroup of spruces at the tree-line

The relic Swiss pine coniferous forest *Cembro-Piceetum* appears in a narrow band close to the tree-line, mainly in the eastern part of the Tatras. The loose forest stands are composed of the Swiss stone pine *Pinus cembra* and the Norway spruce *Picea abies* with a small proportion of the bare-leaved mountain ash *Sorbus aucuparia var. glabrata* and the Carpathian birch *Betula carpatica*. The shrub layer includes the willow *Salix silesiaca*, the dwarf mountain pine *Pinus mugo*, the rock red currant *Ribes petraeum* and the alpine rose *Rosa pendulina*. The undergrowth includes three species of billbery, *Homogyne alpina*, the reed grass *Calamagrostis villosa*, the stiff club-moss *Lycopodium annotinum, Athyrium distentifolium* and the lesser twayblade *Listera cordata*. The largest Swiss pine coniferous forest in the Polish Tatras, measuring some 70 ha in area, has survived in the Żabie region close to Morskie Oko. On the ridge of Czuba Roztocka and on its northern precipices, there are several dozen Swiss pine

Edelweiss

Milk-weed gentian

Red bilberry

Green spleenwort

clumps, which together with some larches form a well preserved, relic Swiss pine and larch coniferous forest, which has probably survived here since the warm interglacial periods in the Pleistocene.

The plant association growing at the tree-line plays a major role by protecting the forest stands below it from snow and rock avalanches as well as winds, in particular the *halny* foehn wind. The tree-line in the Tatras is a vegetation belt whose width varies from one to several dozen metres. Its floral composition depends on the local habitat conditions and shows major differences over short distances. The elevation of the upper tree-line varies greatly, depending on the local orographic conditions, the impact of natural process- es – for example, snow avalanches in concave landforms have pushed forests down, and former grazing, which in some regions has even caused this natural formation to disappear completely.

The tree-line in the vicinity of Hala Gąsienicowa

Forest clearings are an interesting landscape feature of forest belts in the Tatras. They are mainly found in lower sub-alpine forests, but some reach the upper sub-alpine forest up to the elevation of 1,350 m a.s.l. Tatra clearings are most frequently covered by the semi-natural meadow plant association of *Gladiolus imbricatus* and the bent grass *Gladio-lo-Agrostietum* which is considered to be endemic to the Western Tatras. It is characterised by the occurrence of up to 70 vascular plants, of which some 95% are native species. This association has developed as a secondary one in places where men have felled the forest and can survive only thanks to continuous fertilisation, mowing and grazing of the meadows. Otherwise, they will become overgrown by forest again. In order to protect these biologically rich ecosystems, a limited, "cultural" sheep grazing is permitted on selected Tatra clearings, while other clearings are subject to active protection, e.g. mowing. The characteristic meadow plant species found in the *Gladiolus imbricatus* and bent grass association are the ubiquitous lady's-mantle *Alchemilla*, mainly *Alchemilla walasii* and the violet *Viola saxatilis var. decorata*. Here, one can also often find *Gladiolus imbricatus*, the bent grass *Agrostis capillaris*, the cornflower *Centaurea oxylepis* and its hybrid with *C. jacea*. During the growing season, we can observe very characteristic, beautiful cycles of subsequent phenological stages on Tatra clearings. While the snow is still melting or has just disappeared, the saffron *Crocus scepusiensis* often blooms in masses, and its violet flowers cover whole swathes of meadows in this colour. In late May, the meadows start becoming predominantly white with the flowers of large swathes of *Cardaminopis halleri*

A saffron-covered clearing at the foot of the Tatras

and the stitchwort *Stellaria graminea*. In July, when the clearings reach their full summer development, the meadows are adorned with the purple-violet flowers of *Gladiolus imbricatus*. The last plant to flower in groups, although not in all clearings, is the meadow saffron *Colchicum autumnale*. It blooms in late August and September. Because of the similarity of its colour and flower appearance to the common saffron it is often confused with the latter, although it belongs to the lily family (*Liliaceae*), while the saffron is part of the iris family *Iridaceae*.

On some meadows very intensively used by man, e.g. in the vicinity of mountain lodges, shepherds' huts, under former sheep pens, or next to tourist trails, other plant communities have developed. Those are synanthropic associations growing on habitats overfertilised with nitrogen compounds. The characteristic plant species common in them are the monk's rhubarb *Rumex alpinus* and *R. obtusifolius*, the tussock-grass *Poa annua ssp. varia* and the speedwell *Veronica serpyllifolia*.

The Tatra forests are an important living habitat for animals. Among the mammals, many species currently living in the Tatras used to inhabit lowland primeval forests. At present, the Tatras have retained the following predators: the wolf *Canis lupus*, the lynx *Lynx lynx*, the fox *Vulpes vulpes*, the pine marten *Martes martes*, the ermine *Mustella erminea*, the otter *Lutra lutra*, the weasel *Mustela nivalis* and the brown bear *Ursus arctos*. This largest forest predator, once hunted almost to extinction, has now increased its population to over a dozen specimens. Meeting a bear is no longer a sensation. The red deer *Cervus elaphus* and the roe deer *Capreolus capreolus* are common in the forests, while wild boars *Sus scrofa* appear at the periphery of the Tatras. Small rodents are also common in forests and on clearings, including the brown-black form of the squirrel *Sciurus vulgaris*, the forest dormouse *Dryomys nitedula* and the common dormouse *Muscardinus avellanarius*. However, the most numerous rodent in the Tatras is the bank vole *Clethrionomys glareolus*, with up to 10.7 specimens per hectare. During seed years, when the amount of available food increases, the numbers of these rodents can rise as much as tenfold. A very interesting animal that can be found in the Tatras is one of the rarest Polish rodents – the northern birch mouse *Sicista betulina*. Of insectivorous mammals, the hedgehog *Erinaceus concolor* is rather rare in the sub-alpine forests. The mole *Talpa europaea* is also relatively infrequent but reaches up to the mountain pasture belt. On the other hand, the common shrew *Sorex araneus* is common in forests and on clearings, and it is found from the foot of the Tatras up to the fell belt. The lesser shrew *S. minutus* is also present in all belts, unlike the alpine shrew, often distinguished as a separate subspecies *S. alpinus tatricus*, which lives mainly in the upper parts of the sub-alpine forest belt. Of other insectivorous mammals, the European water-shrew can be found by streams up to the dwarf mountain pine belt, while the Mediterranean water-shrew is much less frequent. Several species of bats (*Chiroptera*) inhabiting Tatra forests and clearings include the brown bat *Myotis myotis*, the northern bat *Eptesicus nilssonii* and the common long-eared bat *Plecotus auritus*. In the autumn, these insectivorous mammals hide in tree-hollows and caves, where they hibernate throughout the winter. The bats hibernating in Tatra caves include species that are rare and endangered in Poland.

The varied beech and fir tree stands and old growth spruce forests are a haven for birds. Some 65 species build their nests in lower sub-alpine forests, with 69 bird pairs on every

A forest clearing under economic use

A deer in the forest

Chaffinch

Great spotted woodpecker

Eagle owl

Tengmalm's owl

Dipper

Ptarmigan

The Toporowy Staw Lake

10 hectares. The dominant birds are chaffinches *Fringilla coelebs*, robins *Erithacus rubecula*, wood warblers *Phylloscopus sibilatrix* and coal tits *Parus ater*. Far fewer birds are observed in the upper sub-alpine spruce coniferous forests. About 35 species nest here, and the number of pairs per 10 ha is 36. Apart from the chaffinches and robins which dominate the bird fauna of the Tatras, here one finds species that prefer coniferous forests: the goldcrest *Regulus regulus*, the hedge accentor *Prunella modularis*, the ring ousel *Turdus torquatus* and the crested tit *Parus cristatus*. In spruce and spruce-Swiss pine coniferous forests, one can also observe a species very infrequent in Poland: the three-toed woodpecker *Picoides tridactylus*. Birds of prey found here include: the goshawk *Accipiter gentilis*, the sparrow hawk *A. nisus* and the buzzard *Buteo buteo*, while nocturnal birds living here are the eagle owl *Bubo bubo* and the Tengmalm's owl *Aegolius funereus*. Forests at higher elevations are the nesting place of large gallinaceous birds: the woodgrouse *Tetrao urogallus*, the black grouse *Tetrao tetrix* and the hazel grouse *Tetrastes bonasia*. The grey wagtail *Motacilla cinerea* and the dipper *Cinclus cinclus* can be found near Tatra waters.

The sub-alpine forest belt is inhabited by a relatively numerous ovoviviparous reptile – the adder *Vipera berus*, which can be grey, brown or black in colour, while wet habitats at lower elevation are also inhabited by other reptile and amphibian species, including the rare spotted salamander *Salamandra salamandra*, the alpine newt *Triturus alpestris*, the Carpathian newt *Triturus montandoni* (endemic to the Carpathians) and the common newt *Triturus vulgaris*, whose highest location in Poland is found in the Toporowy Staw Niżni lake. Tailless amphibians include the yellow-bellied toad *Bombina variegata* – a mountain species frequently found in the lower sub-alpine forests – and the common frog *Rana temporaria*.

Various habitats in the sub-alpine forests, and particularly forest clearings, sunny rock outcrops and scree fields, as well as streams and other bodies of water are the home of many invertebrate species, of which insects are the most numerous group. Those well represented here include wingless insects *Apterygota,* butterflies *Lepidoptera,* beetles *Coleoptera,* dipterans *Diptera,* homopterans *Homoptera* heteropterans *Heteroptera,* mayflies *Ephemerida,* caddis flies *Trichoptera* and other insect orders. However, the species one finds here are mainly those living all over the Carpathians and also in the lowlands.

The dwarf mountain pine belt

The dwarf mountain pine belt in the Tatras is located above the upper sub-alpine forest, between the altitudes of 1,500 and 1,800 m a.s.l. The climate conditions prevailing

Continuous fields of dwarf mountain pine

here are characteristic of the very cool climate belt, where the average annual temperature hovers about 0°C and the annual precipitation reaches 1,800 mm. In this belt there is more snow than rain. Winter lasts for some 182 days in a year here and snow lies for 215 days on the average.

At first, close to the tree-line, this belt is dominated by a continuous brushwood of the dwarf mountain pine *Pinus mugo* which can be up to 3 m tall. As one climbs higher, the fields of dwarf mountain pine become more sparse, so at the upper limit one finds only small clumps of this pine, no higher than a dozen centimeters. With increase in altitude, the dwarf mountain pine is gradually replaced by mountain pastures. The dwarf mountain pine, together with other shrubs and undergrowth plants forms the association of *Pinetum mughi carpaticum.*

Apart from the pine, this association includes the mountain ash *Sorbus aucuparia,* the willow *Salix silesiaca*, the rock red currant *Ribes petraeum*, the bird cherry *Padus petraea*, the alpine rose *Rosa pendulina,* and in the Eastern Tatras, the Carpathian birch *Betula carpatica.* The undergrowth layer is most frequently comprised of ferns: the scented fern *Dryopteris expansa* and *Athyrium distentifolium*, as well as *Homogyne alpina*, the greater wood rush *Luzula sylvatica, Leucanthemum waldsteinii*, the reed grass *Calamagrostis villosa* and billberries: the black *Vaccinium myrtillus* and red *V. vitis-idaea.*

Wet habitats in the dwarf mountain pine belt are covered by varied and species-rich herb associations. These characteristic associations usually grow at the borders of scree fields, at the feet of rock walls, on wide rock shelves and by streams. They differ from one another because of the location, the nature of the bedrock and the ground moisture level. One of them is *Adenostyletum alliariae*, which is dominated by *Adenostyles alliarie, Mulgedium alpinum* and the Austrian leopard's-bane *Doronicum austriacum.* The numerous other perennial plants found in this association are: the wood cranesbill *Geranium silvaticum, Leucanthemum waldsteinii*, the ragwort *Senecio nemorensis,* the willow herb *Epilobium alpestre* and the milkweed gentian *Gentiana asclepiadea.* Similar habitats but on a limestone bedrock are covered by the association of the monkshood *Aconitetum firmi*, with its characteristic species *Aconitum firmum*, larkspurs *Delphinium oxysepalum* and *D. elatum,* as well as the garden angelica *Archangelica officinalis.*

Dryer habitats are overgrown by lush and species-rich grass associations. If the bedrock is not limestone, the Tatra association of the reed grass *Calamagrostietum villosae tatricum* grows up to the alpine pasture belt at the elevation of about 2,200 m. It can be identified by the fresh green colour of the tall reed grass *Calamagrostis villosa.* Apart from the reed grass, this association includes another grass – the fescue *Festuca picta*, and

Monkshood

Spotted gentian

Leopard's bane

Awens

Garden angelica

Bluebell

Sengreen

Yellow vetch

Narcissus anemone

Primrose

plants like the gentian *Gentiana punctata, Gnaphalium norvegicum,* the mixed-flower *Phyteuma spicatum,* a mountain form of the goldenrod *Solidago virga-aurea ssp. alpestris* and the hawkweed *Hieracium alpinum.*

The same habitats on a limestone bedrock are covered by the aforementioned fescue association *Festucetum carpaticae* which is found mainly in the dwarf mountain pine belt, but can also grow as low as the upper sub-alpine forest and as high as on the highest limestone peaks. With increasing altitude, the composition of this association changes slightly.

The dwarf mountain pine belt constitutes an intermediate region between the forest belts and the typical high mountain environment. The limits of altitude of many plant and animal species occur here. Gradually but clearly, the number of species that are common in lower habitats decreases here, while specialised species characteristic of high mountain areas appear with increasing frequency.

Among the mammals, this belt is dominated by small rodents including the common shrew *Sorex araneus,* the lesser shrew *S. minutus,* the forest dormouse *Dryomys nitedula,* the common dormouse *Muscardinus avellanarius* and the bank vole *Clethrionomys glareolus.* Several species of bats rare in Poland can frequently be found in caves. Various species of carnivorous mammals also reach here, including the brown bear *Ursus arctos,* the lynx *Lunx lynx* and the fox *Vulpes vulpes.* This belt also already affords one the opportunity of meeting the typical Tatra mammals: the chamois *Rupicapra rupicapra tatrica* and the alpine marmot *Marmota marmota.*

The intermediate zone between the upper sub-alpine coniferous forest and the dwarf mountain pine belt forms the upper limit of the majority of forest species. In the dwarf mountain pine zone, we find only 10 species of nesting birds, whose density is 5 pairs per 10 ha. Species from the alpine zone appear here: the water pipit *Anthus spinoletta* and the hedge accentor *Prunella modularis.* They account for almost 85% of all individual birds living in this environment. In this belt, one can also find the black redstart *Phoenicurus ochruros* which is also common in lowlands, as well as the tundra form of the bluethroat *Luscinia svecica svecica* and the boreal/alpine redpoll *Acanthis flammae cabaret.*

Of reptiles and amphibians, only the scaly lizard *Lacerta vivipara,* the common northern viper *Vipera berus,* the alpine newt *Triturus alpestris* and the common grass frog *Rana temporaria* venture as high as to the dwarf mountain pine belt.

The fauna of insects living here, although much more limited, includes high mountain species: butterflies like ringlet butterflies *Erebia epiphron* and *E. manto, Boloria pales* and many geometers, beetles: *Carabus transsylvanicus, Nebrica tatrica* and *Deltomerus tatricus* and mountain species of bumblebees: *Bombus elegans, B. mastucatus* and *B. pyrenaeus.*

The mountain pasture and fell belt

Above the dwarf mountain pine brushwood, lies the mountain pasture belt, also referred to as the alpine belt. On limestone bedrock, it stretches from some 1,800 m above sea level to the highest peaks. In the area built of crystalline rocks, it reaches up to an elevation of 2,200–2,300 m a.s.l. The climatic conditions prevailing here are characteristic for a moderately cold climatic zone, where the average annual temperature is about -2°C and the annual precipitation to 1,750 mm. There is more snow than rain in this zone.

The mountain pasture belt

Winter lasts for some 215 days in the year here and snow covers the ground for some 250 days on average.

The vegetation of this belt is of a distinct high mountain character. A zone of high mountain grassland stretches above the dwarf mountain pine brushwood. If the bedrock is granite, the dominant association is that of the rush and *Oreochloa disticha (Oreochloo distichae-Juncetum trifidi)* which is a climate-determined, permanent, natural association characteristic of this climatic zone in the non-limestone mountain areas of Europe. The basic species belonging to this formation are the rush *Juncus trifidus* which forms a thick, rigid turf, and the thick tussock-forming grass *Oreochloa disticha*. The narrow leaves of the

The fell belt

rush dry out and turn red in the early autumn, giving a characteristic reddish colour to entire granite peaks. It is for this colour that Czerwone Wierchy (literally: the Red Peaks) have been named. Apart from these species, this plant association also includes the fescue *Festuca supina*, the anemone *Pulsatilla alba*, the ragwort *Senecio carpaticus*, *Avenastrum versicolor*, the hawkweed *Hieracium alpinum* and the primrose *Primula minima*.

The woodrush association *Luzuletum spadiceae* forms low grasslands with a small proportion of bryophytes in moist areas and in places where patches of snow survive for a longer time on a granite bedrock. This association reaches up to the highest Tatra peaks. It is named after the woodrush *Luzula spadicea* which dominates it. This plant is accompanied by a grass endemic to the Carpatians – the tussock grass *Poa granitica*, and the leopard's bane *Doronicum clusii*, the buttercup *Ranunculus montanus*, and *Oligotrichum hercynicum* representing the bryophytes.

Areas of limestone bedrock in the mountain pasture belt are covered by two clearly different grassland associations. One is the sedge association *Caricetum firmae carpaticum* which grows in rocky places covered with a very thin layer of soil. This association is dominated by the sedge *Carex firma* with very rigid, dark green leaves. It is accompanied by the mountain avens *Dryas octopetala*. Another characteristic feature of this association are the dense cushions of the saxifrage *Saxifraga caesia*. One can also see the smallest orchid *Chamaeorchis alpina*, *Crepis jacquini*, the rock rose *Helianthemum alpestre* and the violet *Viola alpina* here. What is also very characteristic is the occurrence of the yellow lichen *Cetraria tilesii* found between the above plants.

Tall alpine grasslands on thicker, calcareous soils rich in humus and sometimes slightly neutralised or acidified are formed by a fescue association *Festuco versicoloris-Seslerietum tatrae*. This association is named for the dominant species: the fescue *Festuca versicolor* and *Sesleria tatrae*.

A very specific environment for vegetative cover is provided by *wyleżyska*. These are parts of high mountain cirques where the snow remains for a particularly long time and often only melts at the end of July. Such areas are overgrown by different plant associations, depending on the type of bedrock and the duration of snow cover. These associations often grow both in the mountain pasture belt and in the dwarf mountain pine belt, and sometimes even also in the fell belt. Where the snow lies the longest, up to 10 months, only the pioneering bryophyte association of *Polytrichetum sexangularis*, named for the dominant haircup moss *Polytrichum sexangularis*, grows. If the snow cover lasts for a shorter time, an association of the dwarf willow *Salicetum herbaceae* develops. Almost all plants on *wyleżyska* are tiny, usually spread flat close to the ground. The dominant species is the dwarf willow *Salix herbacea* for which the above association is named. In addition, we also find *Cerastium trigynum* and *Gnaphalium supinum*. In *wyleżyska* overgrowing stabilised, fine-grained limestone grit, a saxifrage association *Saxifragetum perdurantis* endemic to the Tatras has developed.

A highly specific plant cover is also seen on scree cones found at the feet of rock walls.

The highest vegetation belt in the Tatras is the fell belt, also referred to as the subnival belt. It usually starts at 2,200 – 2,300 m above sea level and is therefore fully developed only in the granite High Tatras. The climatic conditions prevailing here are characteristic of the cold climate zone. The average annual temperature is -4°C and the total annual precipitation amounts to some 1,625 mm. On the average, the winter lasts here for as long as 245 days, and snow lies on the ground for 290 days. However, even in these severe climatic conditions, some 120 species of flowering plants and pteridophytes grow on the highest, granite peaks.

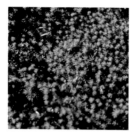

Haircup moss

Pink

Anemone

Catchfly

Rose root

Tufts of loose grassland of the fell association *Oreochloëtum distichae subnivale* grow among rock walls usually covered only with lichen. These tufts are found up to the upper limit of flowering plants. They are dominated by *Oreochloa disticha*, while the characteristic species include: the gentian *Gentiana frigida*, the woodrush *Luzula spicata*, *Minuartia sedoides*, the ragwort *Senecio carniolicus* and a subspecies of the catchfly *Silene acaulis* which grows only on granite. Apart from this association, the fell belt also features low grasslands with a small proportion of bryophytes that cover humus-rich, stabilised limestone grits on the slopes, in places where the snow-cover lasts for a long time. This association is called *Luzuletum spadiceae*. The species found in it most frequently is the woodrush *Luzula spadicea*, the tussock grass *Poa granitica* and the buttercup *Ranunculus montanus*.

The special conditions of the high mountain climate cause a number of adaptations in plants. These include cushion forms of plants, turf plants, concentric circle growth of plants, low row shrubs, plants covered in hairs, viviparous and insectivorous plants.

In the highest parts of the Tatras, apart from flowering plants, one finds numerous species of bryophytes and lichens, particularly ones growing on rocks and therefore very well adjusted to the extreme vegetation conditions prevailing here.

The highest climate and vegetation belts of the Tatras are home to high mountain animals found nowhere else in Poland. They include the symbol of the Tatra National Park – the chamois *Rupicapra rupicapra tatrica,* and the alpine marmot *Marmota marmota.* The chamois live in herds of several animals. Old males (goats) live alone and join the herds only during the rut, which lasts from September to November. In total, only a little over 110 animals of this species have been counted in the Polish part of the Tatras. The alpine marmot is a very characteristic rodent species found in Poland only in the Tatras. Its population consists of some 190 specimens. Like the majority of high mountain animals it is active during the day, and spends the night in the burrows it digs. As the marmot hibernates through the winter in its underground burrows, it can survive the unfavourable weather conditions and the resulting lack of food. Another high mountain rodent is the snow vole *Microtus niwalis.* Unlike the marmot, it does not dig burrows but finds shelter among rocks and boulders. It is active both during the day and night. It does not even hibernate, but leads an active life in the winter burrowing under the snow. The third high mountain rodent, the Tatra pine vole *Pitymys tatricus* is very secretive and spends a lot of time in the burrows it digs.

Only a few bird species occur in the highest parts of the Tatras, in the mountain pasture and fell belts. In the mountain

A chamois with a foal

Alpine marmot

Snow vole

Golden eagle

Alpine accentor

pasture belt, their density does not exceed 7 pairs per 10 ha. The 7 or 8 species found in the highest parts of the mountain pasture belt include almost only those typical of mountain areas. The most frequent are the water pipit *Anthus spinoletta* and the alpine accentor *Prunella collaris*. Only 4 bird species build nests in the fell belt: the golden eagle *Aquila chrysaetos*, the kestrel *Falco tinnunculus*, the raven *Corvus corax* and the wallcreeper *Tichodroma muraria*.

There are also only a few high mountain invertebrate species found in the highest zones of the Tatras. Among the butterflies, these include ringlets: *Erebia epiphron*, *E. manto*, *E. gorge*, *E euryale* and *E. pandrose*, *Boloria pales* and numerous geometers *Geometridae*, of which the small, grey *Psodos canaliculata* is characteristic of the highest parts. Among the beetles: the common *Carabus transsylvanicus* and *Nebrica tatrica*, *Deltomerus tatricus*, *Pterostichus negligens* and the very rare ladybird *Semiadalia alpina redtenbacheri*. The remaining orders are poorly represented on the Tatra peaks.

74

IV. Historic and present threats

The unique natural and cultural treasures of the Polish Tatras, recognised by the establishment of the national park, were in the past and still are subject to various threats.

The reckless exploitation of natural resources, and particularly the excessive felling of trees and overgrazing have significantly changed the primeval environment of the Tatras. The felling of forests for the requirements of mining, smelting, grazing and the wood industry have caused significant deforestation, while misguided forest management in the late 19th and early 20th centuries resulted in artificial spruce monocultures on the rich biotopes of beech and fir forests in a significant proportion of the lower sub-alpine forest. Overgrazing has significantly pushed down the tree-line and initiated erosion processes in the upper parts of the mountains. Poaching always has and still constitutes a certain threat, particularly to rare or unusual animal species, such as the alpine marmot or the chamois.

Areas where the natural environment has been most altered by past, erroneous economic use have been classified for partial protection. Here, it is necessary to apply active protection measures. These include measures aimed at restoring damaged forest stands to their primeval form and thus to raise their resistance to damaging factors. Measures are also undertaken to stop anthropogenic erosion and maintain biodiversity on non-forest areas.

However, in the end of the 20th century, new, even more serious threats appeared, which could lead to the total degradation of the Park's natural life. These new threats are air pollution and the resulting acid rains, soil and water contamination as well as excessive mass tourism. Fortunately, the first group of threats caused by air pollution no longer poses a major hazard to the Tatras as man has started paying more attention to keeping the natural environment clean.

At present, one of the major threats to the nature of the Tatra National Park is the excessive tourist traffic. In every recent year, almost 3 million tourists have visited the Tatras.

Such a great number of people on Tatra trails means that they get trampled, and this accelerates natural erosion processes. The concentration of people in more interesting spots, like vista points, causes a significant trampling of the ground, which can be seen on the Sucha Przełęcz Pass near Kasprowy Wierch as well as in other places in the Tatras. The huge amounts of trash, waste and food scraps left in the mountains also pose a significant threat. Every year, over 2,000 m^3 of compacted waste is removed from the Park. Waste left in the mountains not only destroys their beauty, but also attracts animals looking for readily available food. Consequently, many animal species found in the Park are becoming synanthropic. A bear looking for food among tourists is just one example of this dependence of animals on humans that can be hazardous to both. The plant cover is also becoming synanthropic, particularly near buildings and the busier trails. Mountain lodges with restaurants,

Slope erosion caused by past grazing

The trampling of trails activates the erosion processes

which are located in almost every valley, contribute to contaminating the water of Tatra streams. Fortunately, the majority of them now operate fairly efficient sewage treatment plants. A new effort which has only been started in recent years is to prevent the contamination of the ground along the most popular tourist trails with faeces. For this purpose, portable toilets have been provided in selected spots in the Park. One example for the scale of this problem is that at the height of the season, the Morskie Oko Lake is visited by over ten thousand people every day, with the trip taking several hours. Other threats to Tatra nature caused by the excessive tourist traffic include excessive noise which disturbs and frightens animals in their natural refuges as well as frequent breaches of the regulations and limits in force within the Tatra National Park.

For many years, the Polish Tatra National Park (TPN) has enjoyed a good relationship with the Slovak Tatras National Park (TANAP) on the other side of the border. Even though our two parks are separated by a national border, they cover the entire Tatras, which form an indivisible natural entity. Consequently, they both face very similar protection problems, apply similar protective strategies and tactics and have undertaken joint initiatives and actions since their very inception, or even earlier. This co-operation is developing and allows us to solve current problems better, but in the face of the increasing global threats, an even broader international co-operation is necessary.

In 1993, a biosphere reserve was established on the entire area of the Tatras. The proposal for this reserve was the result of several years of co-operation by specialists from both sides of the national border. The reserve was divided into zones according to the results of an inventory-taking of the nature and an assessment of the degree of degradation

Mass tourism

The Slovak Tatras

and danger in the Tatra region. The reserve was designed so that its individual zones complement one another and form a reasonable spatial arrangement. The Tatra Biosphere Reserve measures 145,600 ha in area, with 20,400 ha on the Polish and 125,200 ha on the Slovak side. Agreements have also been reached and work undertaken to unify the subjects and methods of research, monitoring and protective activities in both national parks. The Tatra Biosphere Reserve now forms a part of the international network of biosphere reserves which cover the main types of ecosystems in the world. The purpose of biosphere reserves is to make the most valuable natural ecosystems of our globe available for comparative scientific studies. The participation of the Polish and Slovak Tatra National Parks in the international MaB programme will allow us, to a greater extent than previously, to take advantage of other countries' experience in effective nature protection and to improve the organisation and forms of activities necessary to protect the nature of the Tatras.

Bibliography

Bac-Moszaszwili M., Gąsienica-Szostak M., *Tatry Polskie. Przewodnik geologiczny dla turystów (The Polish Tatras. A Geological Handbook for Tourists)*. WG, Warszawa, 1990.

Cichocki W., Siarzewski W., *Walory przyrodnicze Tatr (Natural Values of the Tatras)*. [in]: „Tytus Chałubiński – Tatry" Radom, 1995.

Głowaciński Z., *Znajomość i ogólna charakterystyka fauny (The Identification and General Characteristics of the Fauna)*. [in]: Z. Mirek *et al. (ed.)* Przyroda Tatrzańskiego Parku Narodowego (The Nature of the Tatra National Park), TPN, Kraków–Zakopane, 1996.

Hess M., *Klimat (Climate)*. [in]: Z. Mirek *et al. (ed.)* Przyroda Tatrzańskiego Parku Narodowego (The Nature of the Tatra National Park), TPN, Kraków–Zakopane, 1996.

Klimaszewski M., *Rzeźba Tatr Polskich (The Relief of the Polish Tatras)*. PWN, Warszawa, 1988.

Kot M., Krzan Z., Siarzewski W., Skawiński P., *Tatrzański Park Narodowy (The Tatra National Park)*. Warszawa, 1993.

Mirek Z., Piękoś-Mirkowa H., *Rośliny kwiatowe i paprotniki (Flower Plants and Pteridophytes)*. [in]: Z. Mirek *et al. (ed.)* Przyroda Tatrzańskiego Parku Narodowego (The Nature of the Tatra National Park), TPN, Kraków–Zakopane, 1996.

Piękoś-Mirkowa H., Mirek Z., *Zbiorowiska roślinne (Plant Associations)*. [in]: Z. Mirek *et al. (ed.)* Przyroda Tatrzańskiego Parku Narodowego (The Nature of the Tatra National Park), TPN, Kraków–Zakopane, 1996.

Piękoś-Mirkowa H., Mirek Z., *Ochrona różnorodności gatunkowej flory Tatr. 1. Endemity (Protection of the Flora Species Diversity of the Tatras. 1. Endemic taxa)*. [in]: W. Borowiec *et al. (ed.)* Przemiany środowiska przyrodniczego Tatr (Transformations of the Tatra Natural Environment), TPN, PTPNoZ, Kraków–Zakopane, 2002.

Piękoś-Mirkowa H., Mirek Z. *(Protection of the Flora Species Diversity of the Tatras. 2. Legally Protected Species)*. [in]: W. Borowiec *et al. (ed.)* Przemiany środowiska przyrodniczego Tatr (Transformations of the Tatra Natural Environment), TPN, PTPNoZ, Kraków–Zakopane, 2002.

Piękoś-Mirkowa H., Mirek Z., *Atlas roślin chronionych (The Protected Species Book)*. Mulico, Warszawa, 2003.

Profus P., *Ssaki (Mammals)*. [in]: Z. Mirek *et al. (ed.)* Przyroda Tatrzańskiego Parku Narodowego (The Nature of the Tatra National Park), TPN, Kraków–Zakopane, 1996.

Przyroda Tatrzańskiego Parku Narodowego (The Nature of the Tatra National Park). A collective work edited by Z. Mirek *et al.*, TPN, Kraków–Zakopane, 1996.

Rozporządzenie Rady Ministrów z dnia 1 kwietnia 2003 r. w sprawie TPN (Regulation of the Council of Ministers of 1 April 2003 on the Tatra National Park). Journal of Laws 03.65.599 of 16 April 2003.

Szymczakowski W., *Owady (Insects)*. [in]: Z. Mirek *et al. (ed.)* Przyroda Tatrzańskiego Parku Narodowego (The Nature of the Tatra National Park), TPN, Kraków–Zakopane, 1996.

Ziemońska Z., *O hydrografii Tatr Polskich (On the Hydrography of the Polish Tatras)*. Czasopismo Geograficzne 45, nr 1, 1974.